AIR RAID

AIR RAID

The Technique of Silent
Approach

High Explosive

Panic

by

JOHN LANGDON-DAVIES

LONDON
GEORGE ROUTLEDGE & SONS, LTD.
BROADWAY HOUSE : 68-74 CARTER LANE, E.C.
1938

MADE AND PRINTED IN GREAT BRITAIN
AT GAINSBOROUGH PRESS, ST. ALBANS
BY FISHER, KNIGHT AND CO., LTD.

NOTE

I have to thank S. Argulló of Barcelona for the photographs in this book; my wife for drawing the map and two other figures; Dr. Luis Revilla Martos and other officials of the Junta de Denfensa Passiva de Catalunya for answering all my questions; and Dr. John Rickman for many valuable suggestions. S. Marian Vives was very helpful in collecting witnesses, and Mr. Donald Darling was kind enough to help me in many ways.

DESCRIPTION OF MAP

In this map of Barcelona the three districts seen from the air in Plates II, VIII, IX and XII can be related to the whole city.

A   is the University,

B   the scene of destruction photographed in Plates XIV, XVI, XVIII, XX, XXVI, XXVIII and XXIX,

C   the Coliseum,

D   Oro del Rhin Restaurant,

E   the Novetats Theatre destroyed (see page 53),

F   the bomb in the Plaza Tetuan,

G   the bomb at the corner of P. de Catalunya,

H   the bomb at Hotel Colon,

K   the corner opposite Coliseum destroyed by the bomb (Plate XVIII),

L   the bomb in the Calle de Balmes,

M   the position shown destroyed in Plates XXII and XXIII,

N   the house shown in Plate III,

P   the bomb shown in Plate XVII,

X,X,X, the thirteen bombs that fell approximately at 2 p.m.

It will be noted that Barcelona has a far less difficult transport problem than London and that much of it consists of geometrically planned roads at right angles. Consider the traffic difficulties that might be caused by a similar raid on London by imagining Trafalgar Square superimposed on the Plaza de Catalunya; Piccadilly Circus would be near the Ronda de Universidad in front of A, and the Corts Catalanes would be Piccadilly.

The impossibility of distinguishing military objectives is clearly shown. Thus the harbour is seen in close proximity to the thickly populated working-class district in the right-hand lower corner.

Between Paral-lel and Ramblas is the workers' Fifth District, itself free of all military objectives but in close proximity to the power-station to the left of the Paral-lel.

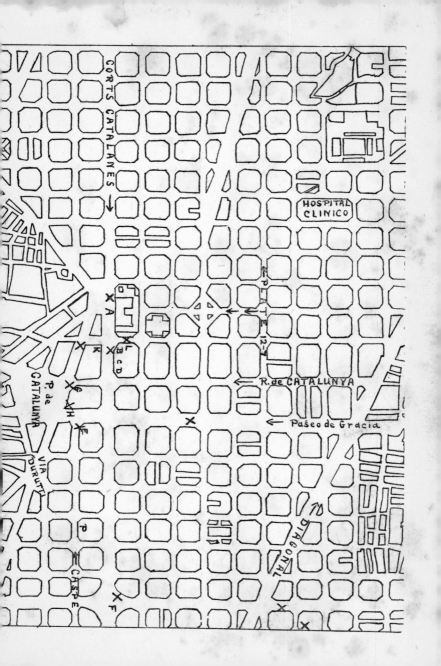

AIR RAID

PART I

THE TECHNIQUE OF SILENT APPROACH

I

THE object of this book is technical. There are certain observed facts about air-bombardment of open cities and the protection of civilian populations which should be borne in mind by our government; since we are a democratic country, this involves putting the facts before the general public.

It is not a book of political propaganda. Indeed, I am aware that the facts that it contains may be used to support political points of view to which I am opposed, as well as others with which I happen to agree. That is neither here nor there.

A member of His Majesty's Government recently observed that when the Spanish

Civil War was over Britain would be the country best-loved by the Spaniards, since we had least interfered with their affairs. That is as may be; but this isolation from any intervention except non-intervention has had one grave disadvantage for the British people: whereas other nations have profited by the opportunities for technical research afforded by the Spanish target, we have gained scarcely any new knowledge about modern weapons of offence and defence. The British people is not aware of some of the most important lessons to be learned, vital as they are to its own future.

There is, of course, a limit to the usefulness of Spain for this purpose. As far as military operations in the field are concerned we can easily be misled by events in Spain. Neither side has adequate resources of men or material to fight a 'real war.' But thanks to the Italo-German manœuvres over Barcelona on March 16th-17th-18th, 1938, we can make a very clear analysis of what happens when an air fleet attacks a large population congregated in a city.

The manœuvres were intended to solve a technical problem and also to see how far its solution would be valuable in a future war.

The results amount to a technical revolution, and, as always when the Attack achieves a revolutionary improvement in technique, it now becomes necessary for the Defence to devise new means of neutralizing the improvement.

March 16th-17th-18th in Barcelona made most A.R.P. literature obsolete. The well-produced A.R.P. manuals still on sale in Barcelona streets are contradicted by the ruins amid which they are sold. The charts of the amount of concrete which will stop a high explosive bomb have disappeared for the best of reasons. It is impossible to find anyone taking an interest in gas-masks, far less in gas-proof rooms. The whole conception of what must be done against bombardment has changed.

And to us in England the March manœuvres are of transcendent interest. Unlike Madrid and Gernika, the conditions were of a character to make a comparison with

London possible. There may never be a raid on London, but, if there is, March in Barcelona saw the dress-rehearsal. The Attack has doubtless learned the lessons; it is the object of this book to lay them before the Defence also.

2

At eight minutes past ten on the evening of March 16th, 1938, the sirens of Barcelona sounded an alarm. Between that hour and 3.19 p.m., March 18th, there were thirteen air-raids which produced destruction in every district of Barcelona and in the surrounding towns.

The total casualties were about 3,000 killed, 5,000 hospital cases, and roughly 20,000 minor injuries.*

As mere casualties the numbers are not impressive for a city of more than a million and a half. They are childish compared with those of a three-days' major offensive during the Great War. Yet from the point of view of the Art of War the operation was the most satisfactory and potentially import-

*Private estimate of a member of the government.

14

ant since the beginning of hostilities. *Its interest lies not in the number of people that were killed, but in what happened to those left alive.*

The lessons to be learned are most important in the field of psychology. The object of the manœuvre was itself psychological. The aim was not casualties, but the creation of panic. The technique employed was designed to nullify existing Defence measures against panic. It succeeded.

The raids were not designed to attack or destroy military objectives; indeed the technique deliberately employed made this impossible except by pure accident. Yet they very nearly won the war for the Spanish Rebels.

I was unable to find anyone who did not frankly admit that he was reduced to a state of impotent terror by the end of the period, and careful observers went so far as to suggest that had the technique been used for another forty-eight hours there would have been a total paralysis of the life of the city and of the power to resist.

Indeed, it is something of a mystery why the raids were broken off when their continuance could have achieved so much. The reason cannot have been a technical one. There was no attrition. No machines nor personnel were lost. The cost was not prohibitive. The Defence had contrived no new countermeasures. It would seem that some political cause in the sphere of international diplomacy came into action to terminate the manœuvres, unless the German technicians felt that they had learned all they needed, so that further experiments were purposeless. Or perhaps the continuance of the raids would have taught the English and French too much.

The results, as we have said, were disastrous to the Defence. Could the same technique be applied to London and other English cities ? It is at least desirable for the purposes of this study to assume that the Attack will try, and therefore the Defence must be prepared.

The first step for us is to understand in more detail what happened in Barcelona last March.

3

The countermeasures of the Defence involve action which in a Democracy must have the support and understanding of the public. But the British public is still reluctant to believe that air warfare on civilian populations can ever be used outside places like Abyssinia, or China, or Spain. Many people tend to rely on decent public opinion to prevent indiscriminate bombing of civilians, or at least British civilians. This is fallacious reasoning, since, long before it comes to bombing, decent public opinion will have been neutralized.

Plate I is an example of how easy it will be to eliminate the weakness—from the military point of view—of decent public opinion. It has appeared recently in a German newspaper as an illustration of a 'red bombardment of Salamanca.' Anyone who knows Barcelona can recognize the exact spot on the Diagonal where the child is lying. Indeed, the only 'Red' concerned in the incident is the child itself.

Shortly after the March raids in Barcelona a priest preached in a Convent of the Sacred Heart in America. He suggested to his congregation that they might perhaps have been perturbed at reading that Franco's splendid air-force had killed many women and children in Barcelona. He would explain the real facts: Franco, who was above all things a humanitarian, sent word to the 'Reds' saying that he knew where they kept their munitions and was going to bomb them. He asked that all women and children should be taken away to a place of safety. Instead of doing this the 'Reds' had removed the munitions and filled the place up with women and children simply to try to blacken Franco's name.

There is no doubt that the congregation believed the preacher, and there is no reason to doubt that he believed himself. Experience gives us no hope that public opinion can stop the use of a new and valuable technique of destruction, since propagandists exist to break down prejudices against the new.

4

A.R.P. handbooks in their 'general pre-
faces' state that "the Government would use
every endeavour on an outbreak of war to
secure an undertaking from the enemy not
to use poison gas," as such use is contrary
to the Geneva Gas Protocol of 1925. Although it is not so stated, we may assume
that our government will also make every
effort to secure undertakings against the
bombardment of open cities and their civilian populations, since this is contrary to
international law. Can we hope for anything from this?

There is a very good reason why no dis-
tinction is possible between the bombing of
military objectives and the bombing of
civilian populations. The two are inextricably mixed up.

Plate II shows the harbour of Barcelona
as it appears from the air. Within the limits
of the photo are wharves used to discharge
munitions, a cavalry barracks, certain important war-industries factories and, just out

of sight beyond the top left-hand corner, the electric power station and some army aeroplane hangars.

How can any of these be attacked without the risk of the thickly populated workers' quarter also being threatened? In actual fact hundreds of bombs have fallen within the limits of this scene without once hitting any military objective, although two schools and many houses have been wrecked. Plate III shows the result of bombing the 'legitimate objective' of Barcelona Port.

The earlier air-raids on Barcelona were concentrated on such districts as these with the purely negative result that no military objectives were hit and the population moved out into healthier areas.

In October, 1937, I witnessed an air-raid on Barcelonetta (as this port district is called), which is of some interest for our subsequent study. On that occasion the aeroplanes came very low and even machine-gunned the streets from roof level. This technique was subsequently abandoned for a far more difficult one which increased the difficulty of hitting specific objects and was no more useful for the spreading of panic than the earlier technique would have been had it been extended throughout the whole city.

Why was the later technique substituted? A possible reason is that, whereas it is hardly likely that enemy raiders will ever be able to come down to housetop level in London, the method we are to describe could well be adopted against London in a future war. Once more we get the suspicion that what Barcelona experiences is a succession of experiments in new techniques carried out as pure research rather than as part of an attempt to win a war against the Spanish Government. Little is to be hoped or feared from aviation in the way of destroying specific military objects hidden in large cities. A very intimate knowledge of Barcelona would be required to distinguish military objectives in a district like that shown in Plates VIII and IX. (Actually this part of the old town does not contain a single legitimate military target, which has not saved it from being bombed repeatedly.) To the left of the middle line and at the foot of the plate can be seen a small square joined to the Cathedral steps above by a narrow road; the present condition of the left-hand corner of this square is illustrated in Plates XXII and XXIII. Yet the nearest object of military importance is a mile away.

Even in the country where there is no cover from other buildings a military objective is very difficult to destroy from the air. Plate IV is Culera Bridge, a vital point on the main line to France. It has been bombed repeatedly. It is not protected by anti-aircraft guns, yet the only damage it has sustained—very interesting damage which we shall study later—was the result of an explosion on the mountain-side nearly half a mile away. It is said that the inhabitants of the village of Culera, tired of incessant bombings, have to be restrained from themselves bombing their bridge so as to get undisturbed nights—but this is a *broma*!

No, aircraft have only one useful function in the enemy's civilian rear, and that is the destruction not of objects but of morale. *It is not Woolwich Arsenal or Croydon Aerodrome that will be attacked in a future war but the nerve centres of the man in the street.*

We are forced therefore to the following conclusions:

1. It is useless to hope that public opinion can save us in a future war from any technique proved efficacious in Spain or elsewhere.

2. Our potential enemies have profited by the opportunities afforded by Spain to test out the real value of old and new techniques of aerial bombardment.

3. They have found that very poor results come from trying to bomb military objectives in large towns. They have therefore experimented with the psychological value of large-scale civilian bombardment.

4. In so doing they have not been content with using techniques which, owing to the poor condition of the Barcelona defences, would have been sufficiently deadly for the immediate purpose.

23

Instead they have elaborated new and difficult techniques.

5. The only realistic explanation of their conduct is that they have been chiefly concerned with evolving a technique capable of defeating the present Defence technique of London.

6. They have succeeded. And having succeeded they dropped the problem for others, instead of using their success to bring about a rapid conclusion of the war in Spain.

What, then, is this new technique which is evidently so vitally important for us in England?

5

Many of us have a picture of the sky darkened with ominous wings and the deafening roar of aeroplane engines overhead.

In theory the course of a raid is as follows :

1. Approaching bombers detected by sensitive instruments somewhere between their base and their objective.

2. Air-raid alarm given; population takes shelter.

3. Curtain of air barrage sent up to keep raiders away.
4. Some bombers get through defences and bombs are dropped.
5. Bombers make off with pursuit planes at their tails.
6. All-clear sounded; population goes about its business.

That is a simple picture of an ideal raid on London as it was carried out before 1918, and, as technicians of Defence usually prepare for the last rather than the next war, it is against such a raid that A.R.P. is very largely directed.

In fact, however, it bears no resemblance to any raid in Barcelona to-day, nor, probably, to any raid that London is ever likely to experience in the future. *The Attack, knowing perfectly well that the Defence is preparing for a raid conforming to such a timetable, has been seeking the means of neutralizing all its efforts.* For this purpose it has been experimenting with the *Technique of Silent Approach.*

The March manœuvres were a magnifi-

cent example of successful experimentation :
in the thirteen raids on Barcelona during
that experiment probably no aeroplane was
seen or heard before the bombs actually
dropped.

What does this mean to A.R.P. ?

With that ostrich-like behaviour which
seems a truly international characteristic of
all A.R.P. propaganda, you can buy on the
streets of Barcelona to-day a work entitled
Citizen, what must you do in air warfare?
It describes pictorially a hypothetical raid.
The reader will mark the applicability of
these drawings (Fig. 1) to the classic but
obsolete timetable, its irrelevance to any raid
carried out according to the Technique of
Silent Approach.

At 17.28 aeroplanes are discovered and
signalled by a wayside observer. Two
minutes later a general warning is given to
air defence authorities through the telephone
switchboard. Two minutes after this the
public hears the sirens and all rush to the
shelters or set their houses in order. We
see the Wise family five minutes after the

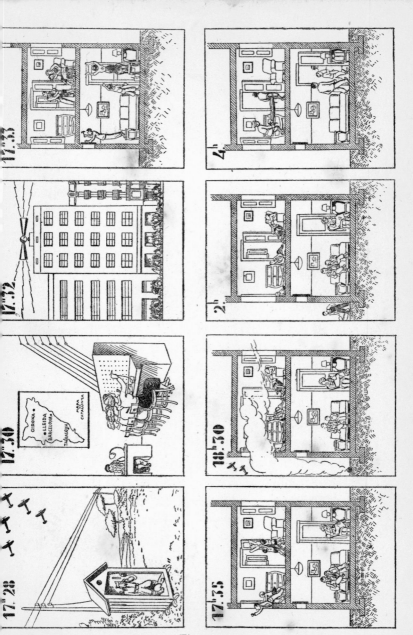

Fig. I

original discovery perfecting their anti-gas room, while the Foolish family begin their inevitable journey towards disaster.

Seven minutes after the discovery, the Wise family are ready and have settled to read the books, which our Home Office memorandum also prescribes as an anti-gas room requisite. The Foolish family are now on the very brink of disaster.

An hour later (the aeroplanes must have been detected over three hundred miles away) an incendiary bomb finishes the Foolishes, while the Wises turn over another page or pearl another stitch.

At 2 a.m. the bucket of sand and spade technique has eliminated the bomb outside, after it has had some six and a half hours to burn. The Wises are still reading, the Foolishes are at rest. At 4 a.m. the sirens blow the all-clear signal, the Wise family sail out under their own power, while their Foolish neighbours are removed to the mortuary. The section of the A.R.P. handbook that contains this scheme is headed "Calma—Calma—Calma."

It may be admitted at once that in London a certain amount of Defence against such an Attack is possible. Given a classic raid, we could deal with it more or less satisfactorily. That is why the Attack has been experimenting with the Technique of Silent Approach.

It is surely significant that as far as Barcelona is concerned the means of combating even a classic raid are so meagre that it might have suited the Italo-German purpose to be content with the classic and straightforward technique. Instead they experimented elaborately with a technique more useful against a heavily protected city like the London of the future, when classic A.R.P. has had time to prepare adequate Defence—against the classic form of Attack.

What, then, is the timetable of a raid carried out in accordance with the Technique of Silent Approach?

6

The pattern worked out during the Italo-German manoeuvres of March 16th-17th-18th over Barcelona conforms to the following timetable:

1. Bombs are heard dropping; people in immediate vicinity not incapacitated seek shelter.

2. (Fifteen-thirty seconds later.) Sirens give air-raid warning; rest of population seek shelter, but with little enthusiasm.

3. (Fifteen seconds later.) Anti-aircraft guns open fire either at direction from which bombs dropped or at aeroplanes which have been sighted, or, since they have now started their engines in readiness for departure, heard.

4. (Twenty seconds later.) Raiders are in full flight and beyond both their objective and the barrage. Nevertheless the barrage continues for perhaps ten minutes and, although all danger is over, terror continues also.

5. (Ten minutes later.) Barrage ceases fire.

6. (Varying time later.) All-clear sounded.

I do not swear that there were no occasions when the bombers were spotted a few seconds before they dropped their bombs, though I believe this to be so, but in no case was there time for the alarmed population to seek shelter. I will go further: *on no occasion did anyone spend a period of danger in a shelter; the shelter was reached when the danger was already passed— unless, of course, a person took up permanent residence at the beginning of the forty hours and remained there until the end.*

The raids came at irregular intervals, and the time between the warning and the all-clear in each raid was as follows: 1 hr. 53 m.; 1 hr. 2 m.; 20 m.; 49 m.; 54 m.; 44 m.; 28 m.; 1 hr.; 37 m.; 26 m.; 33 m.; 28 m.; 19 m. Thus it is possible to draw up the accompanying timetable of how the period was spent by the attacked population.

The first column shows a period of two minutes from the alarm to the end of the period of real danger, assuming that all bombs were dropped within that period. This assumption is legitimate. It appears that in almost every case the real time during which bombs fell from each fleet of raiders was nearer one than two minutes. I have examined the official log very carefully, and the exceptions to this rule can be explained by assuming that another fleet of bombers dropped the later bombs, i.e., that there were two raids in spite of there being only one warning and all-clear. For simplicity, however, these exceptions may be ignored.

The second column shows the period from each of these two-minute periods of real danger until the giving of the all-clear signal. *During this time people are not really in danger, but they think they are.* For the first part of each period anti-aircraft guns are putting up their barrage, in spite of the bombers being already well out of range.

The third column shows the time between the raids. This is at first sight a period of calm without danger, but when we remember that the danger always comes before the alarm, we realize that it is *a period of ever-increasing suspense.* At the beginning people are safe and think they are safe, but as the interval reaches a length which experience suggests to be the average interval between raids the anxiety becomes appalling.

Timetable of Barcelona March manoeuvres from point of view of the Defence

(Beginning 22.08, March 16th; ending 15.19, March 18th)

Raid	2m. Danger and Fear	Fear without Danger	Suspense
A	22.08–22.10	22.10– 0.01 (1h 51m)	0.01– 0.05 (4m)
,, B	0.05– 0.07	0.07– 1.07 (1h 0m)	1.07– 1.36 (29m)
,, C	1.36– 1.38	1.38– 1.56 (18m)	1.56– 7.36 (5h 40m)
,, D	7.36– 7.38	7.38– 8.25 (47m)	8.25–10.26 (2h 1m)
,, E	10.26–10.28	10.28–11.20 (52m)	11.20–13.58 (1h 38m)
,, F	13.58–14.00	14.00–14.42 (42m)	14.42–22.18 (7h 36m)
,, G	22.18–22.20	22.20–22.46 (26m)	22.46– 1.14 (2h 32m)
,, H	1.14– 1.16	1.16– 2.14 (58m)	2.14– 4.03 (1h 49m)
,, I	4.03– 4.05	4.05– 4.40 (35m)	4.40– 7.00 (2h 20m)
,, J	7.00– 7.02	7.02– 7.26 (24m)	7.26– 9.30 (2h 4m)
,, K	9.30– 9.32	9.32–10.03 (31m)	10.03–13.11 (3h 8m)
,, L	13.11–13.13	13.13–13.39 (26m)	13.39–15.00 (1h 21m)
,, M	15.00–15.02	15.02–15.19 (17m)	

c

The forty-odd hours were therefore spent by the populace in a succession of moods which can be summed up as:

(a) thirteen periods of two minutes— danger plus fear;

(b) nine hours and seven minutes of fear without danger;

(c) thirty hours forty-two minutes free of danger, but with growing suspense ending in catastrophe.

In short, *twenty-six minutes of visits from half a dozen bombers themselves scarcely in danger destroyed the whole mental life of a million and a half people for forty hours.* This magnificent result—from the Attack's point of view—was achieved without loss and without deflection of important forces from any military task. How was it done, and could it be repeated on London?

7

Orthodox A.R.P. makes three assumptions:

1. That it is valuable to force the Attack to remain high by the use of barrage and balloon aprons.

2. That the Attack can always be detected in time to get a large portion of the population into reasonable safety.

3. That shelter and the dislocation of life resulting from taking shelter may be regarded as abnormal incidents breaking for brief periods an everyday existence that can be kept otherwise almost normal.

The Technique of Silent Approach makes nonsense of all three assumptions.

The Attack deliberately chooses a high altitude without its efficiency being crippled by the choice.

The Attack evades all detection until after the danger is over.

The Attack is designed to dislocate life for very much longer periods than the raids themselves occupy.

In short, whenever Silent Approach is successful the population cannot get to safety in time and cannot remain in safety for the indefinite period dictated by the Attack.

We come, then, to this conclusion: if the Technique of Silent Approach can be applied

35

*to London, our present A.R.P. methods are
fundamentally unsound. The Attack has set
the Defence an entirely new problem.*

But can London be so treated? Optimists
will be inclined to believe that the success
against Barcelona is due to faulty Defence
there, and that the Defence of London is
already armed against even the new technique of Attack.

This may be true. It is at least certain
that London is mechanically better equipped
to withstand attack than Barcelona, since the
pact of non-intervention has more or less
effectively crippled the Defence from protecting its civilian population. *But a close
analysis of the Barcelona manœuvres shows
that some of the equipment upon which we
rely was available there also and proved
useless.*

There is no doubt at all that the Italo-
German Attack was able to leave its base at
Palma de Mallorca and reach its objective
without being detected. Was this due to
lack of proper equipment on the part of the
Defence?

I was often informed that the aircraft detectors used by the Spanish Government are able to record every aeroplane arriving at or leaving Mallorca, one hundred and twenty-five miles from Barcelona.

This, I believe, was an enthusiastic exaggeration. There are two ways of detecting aeroplanes, by the sound of their engines or by the electro-magnetic effects set up by their engines' rotation. The energy of sound must be totally absorbed within a far shorter radius than one hundred and twenty-five miles—say fifty miles—and the electro-magnetic field set up by the rotating engines is not likely to be detectable at a much greater distance. It is probably safe to say that, unless secret inventions are being used based on principles unknown to most experts, no detector exists capable of detecting a bomber at more than fifty miles. Of course, the shutting off of engines immediately destroys the electro-magnetic form of detection as much as the sound form.

(In passing we may observe that detectors sensitive enough to detect the engines of all

37

planes within a radius of this order might very well be too sensitive for practical use in a major war involving the manœuvring of thousands of planes within that radius.)

In spite of these detectors the bombers arrive over Barcelona without being detected.

The March manœuvres were evidently intended to study the problem of over-coming the most sensitive detectors. How was this done?

The bombers rise from their base to a great height and then glide with engines shut off until their objective is reached. Thus sound detection becomes impossible and, provided a sufficient height is maintained to avoid visual detection, the Technique of Silent Approach is successful.

The distance the bombers can glide is dependent on various factors, including their weight, their best gliding speed, and the angle at which they can glide best.

At the end of the World War the optimum angle was about one in twenty. That is to say, that twenty yards' progress forward could be made for the loss of one yard of altitude.

There is no doubt that great progress has been made since, and a possible best performance for a medium-weight bomber might well be to glide at 120 miles an hour at a gliding angle of one in thirty.

This would mean that such a bomber rising to an initial height of 30,000 feet would glide over a hundred miles while falling to a height of 10,000 feet.

It is no doubt a tremendous problem in human endurance and in mechanical excellence to carry out such a raid, but the figures we have suggested are by no means the upward limit of efficiency possible for this technique. Assuming that the result is likely to be sufficiently valuable to warrant special training and special equipment, an initial height of 45,000 feet could enable bombers to evade detectors and reach their objective at a height above all air barrage; and the number of patrolling pursuit planes needed to detect them would be prohibitive. All the mechanical problems involved have already been solved. *The Defence's problem becomes well-nigh insoluble, not because of mechanical inefficiency, but because the degree of surprise and initiative possessed by the Attack is almost infinite.*

8

What has the Defence got to offer us in the face of this threat of the Technique of Silent Approach? Until an attacking plane has been sighted, the 'active defence' consists of nothing but a balloon curtain, which can merely keep the attackers at a height below which they have no intention of going in any case. The height of an efficient balloon curtain is probably a good deal less than has recently been suggested in the public Press; but in any case the ability of a bomber to rise higher and to remain higher will outstrip the same ability in a captive balloon. After the bombs have dropped, the 'active defence' is the anti-aircraft barrage, which can do little more than make it inconvenient for the bombers to remain any longer than in fact they desire to remain.

Finally, there are the pursuit planes which, to be efficient to protect the population, must be kept flying in sufficient numbers to find the otherwise undetectable attackers and at a sufficient height to give battle to them before they have dropped their bombs. If this is possible (i.e., if at the beginning of a war any country could possess the thousands of pursuit planes necessary), the amount of personnel and machines deflected from the front lines would be crippling.

So much for the 'active defence'; what of the 'passive defence'? That is, what of our system of warnings, shelters, gas masks, gas-proof rooms, air wardens, and the rest of the paraphernalia?

We shall best be able to judge of the adequacy of 'passive defence' after considering the nature of the bombardment carried out by the Attack once it has achieved its initial purpose thanks to Silent Approach.

PART II

HIGH EXPLOSIVE

9

WHAT type of bomb has been used in connection with Silent Approach?

A.R.P. plans in all countries seem to regard gas as the great danger. Gas has not been used in Spain, an abstention which can only be explained in one or other of two ways. Either gas is being saved as a surprise on a future and greater occasion, or gas is not as efficient a weapon as other types of bomb.

It may also be significant that the Defence in most great countries, *but not in Spain,* is already prepared against gas. If gas is the deadly weapon it is often made out to be, and if the object of the attacks on Barcelona is to win the war for Franco, then it seems strange that gas is not being used in

Barcelona, seeing that there are no gas masks or gas-proof rooms there.

If the object of the Italo-German manoeuvres is to experiment with weapons against which A.R.P. in England is unprepared, the omission at once becomes intelligible. However this may be, the reasonable assumption is that, whether or no gas will be used in a future war, it will be used in combination with High Explosive and, of course, incendiary bombs; so that all A.R.P. against gas must also be proof against High Explosive and fire.

The fact remains that in Barcelona the Attack has used no gas, very few incendiary bombs, and that when the Technique of Silent Approach has been adopted nothing but High Explosive has been used.

Very little is known by the general public in England about the effects of High Explosive. Indeed, the long-suffering Spaniards were themselves taken by surprise during the March manoeuvres by what they insist must be a new type of High Explosive with far more appalling results than earlier bombs

44

produced. One of the chief official photographers expressed the general reaction thus: "Don't hope for any photos taken soon after the bombs dropped. I've been bombed in trenches, in Madrid, in Valencia, in Barcelona, before this and taken photos all the time; but when *these* bombs dropped, I found my body running me to the Metro and there I stopped. There were seven of us photographers, and it happened to all of us. You probably can't understand unless you have heard them; anyway, there are no photos immediately after a bombing."

It was impossible to find anyone in Barcelona who was not willing to admit frankly that terror seized him. By the third day the city was in physical flight. Long straggling lines of people carrying their bedding and a few belongings were making for the hills all round. Three long queues stretched into the surrounding streets from the North Station. One man who stood five hours there told me: "As two hours passed from the last raid I began to be sick with terror. There we were near a 'military objective,' the Station, and the time had come for the next raid. I tried to steady myself by thinking, 'If they come, many will run for shelter, and then I will have a better chance of getting a ticket.' But, of course, if they had come, I would have found myself running, too. Fortunately they did not come again, but we did not know that they were not coming."

The crowds in the Metro were such that everybody had to stand all night long for two successive nights wedged body to body. (Yet the Metros are not safe from bombs; people would have been safer in their homes.) For several weeks after, it was necessary to open the trains on one side only, so as to leave the other platforms for the campers who would not leave.

It must not be supposed for a moment that the morale of Barcelona was at the beginning lower than a good average. I saw some dozen or so raids before the March ones, and the impression I got was of a populace which refused to take reasonable care of itself. They would not take shelter. They preferred instead to blacken every balcony

46

so as to get a good view of the bursting shrapnel. Their attitude was the perfectly reasonable one of unprotected people, 'If we are hit, we are hit.' The significant thing about the March raids was that whereas it was just as true as ever that 'If we are hit, we are hit,' people's bodies took them willy-nilly to the horrible atmosphere of the Metro.

In earlier raids people could be seen sitting in stationary tramcars waiting for the raid to be over and the power turned on once more. I have seen old women keep their seats for an hour thus, while others were finishing their drinks in the open-air cafés. Things were different in March. Human reactions then were not even on the level of reasonable fear, nor of reasonable anger against the bombers, or against the Government which could not keep them off. The reactions were on the level of panic.

High Explosive combined with Silent Approach produces panic. Let us first study the material action which causes the psychological breakdown.

47

Just beyond the limits of the older city lies the magnificent broad boulevard called the Corts Catalanes. Plate XII shows part of the new city which lies beyond. The lower

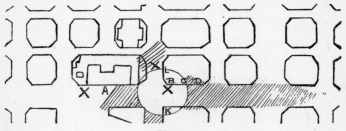

Fig. 2

DETAIL OF BOMB DESTRUCTION BETWEEN
UNIVERSITY AND COLISEUM

The cross marks the crater and the circle the area of total destruction.

The shaded portion shows the area within which passers-by were destroyed by the force of suction. Also at D the part of Oro del Rhin where the people sitting facing the road drinking coffee were killed.

Along the shaded track all glass was destroyed and most windows pushed in. In the other directions the effects were obscured by the two other bombs. Very few of the large blocks of buildings figured escaped considerable injury, while the cross-roads took two weeks to clear.

The width of the Corts Catalanes is about twenty metres and the length of the Coliseum block about one hundred metres.

margin is the Corts, with the University in the centre. On the map at the beginning of the book the relationship of the Corts is seen to the rest of Barcelona. Fig. 2 shows on a

larger scale the block which is only just
visible in the extreme right-hand corner of
Plate XII next the University. The present
condition of this section is clearly seen in
Plates XIV, XVI, XVIII, XX, XXVI,
XXVIII, XXIX.

This destruction has been caused by High
Explosive. So much greater is it than anything that was seen before March that
extravagant stories have been circulating
to explain it. It has been suggested that a
bomb hit a lorry containing TNT, but people
are not in the habit of carrying truck-loads
of this material through the streets of Barcelona. It seems probable that the whole
damage was done by one bomb, although
the possibility cannot be altogether left out
that several were dropped together.

It is also widely assumed in Barcelona
that a new type of explosive was used.
There was no sign of damage from shrapnel,
and small fragments of an aluminium alloy
picked up on the spot are believed to be
remains of the bomb-case; while the belief
is frequently expressed that the explosive

49

D

force was liquid air. Everyone describes the special noise made by 'bombas de aire liquida.' This lay certainty on a technical detail is rather interesting. For some reason 'liquid air' appeals to the imagination. However these things may be, the damage was caused by High Explosive, and is only greater in degree than the damage done elsewhere by the same force. There was no warning except the whistle of the bomb itself.

Here is the official log of the Junta de Defensa Passiva for a part of the raids, from the beginning of the sixth raid to the beginning of the seventh:

13.58 (i.e., 1.58 p.m., March 17th).
The D.E.C.A. instructs us to sound alarm.
We do so at once.
(The D.E.C.A. is the Defensa Especial Contra Aeronaus, that is, the Air Force Department from which the Passive Defence takes its orders.)

13.59 Aerial Observation informs us that the alarm is due to presence of five Rebel aeroplanes.

14.00 We are asked for ambulances from the following places:

New Rambla Street No. 98.

St. John's Avenue No. 104.

Hotel Colon.

Provenza Street No. 365-380.

Plaza de Tetuan.

Paseo de Gracia between Aragon and Consell de Cent.

Balmes St. between Diputacion and Corts.

Corts between Rambla Catalunya and Balmes St.

All these are supplied with military ambulances.

(These eight bombs, as well as the others recorded in the log later, are marked with crosses on the map. We observe that the information about these bombs reached the Defensa within two minutes of the D.E.C.A. instructing them to sound

51

an alarm. We may assume that this short time was needed to get the information from the local air wardens, to make the telephone connections, etc., in fact, that the falling of the bombs was the means whereby the D.E.C.A. became aware of the presence of the five aeroplanes.)

14.25 We inform military ambulances, Red Cross, and local boards that all dead and wounded from the latest bombardment must be taken to the General Hospital.

(This means that the Clinical Hospital and its 'deposit' are full.)

14.31 We are informed that bombs have fallen in the following places: Ronda Universidad, Plaza de Universidad, and Plaza de Catalunya.

(These are probably delayed reports of bombs synchronous with the earlier list.)

14.42 We give 'all-clear' signal.

15.50 We are informed that serious fire has broken out in Carretes Street No. 24. We inform Fire Dept.
(A secondary fire not caused by an incendiary bomb.)

16.35 We are informed that the Novetats Theatre has been destroyed.

19.30 Victims of the last bombardment reported as follows: General Hospital, 80 dead, 229 wounded; Clinical Hospital, 335 dead, 350 wounded.
(Naturally a large number of victims are still being dug out of ruins.)

22.18 The D.E.C.A. instructs us to sound alarm. We do so at once.

It will be seen that the bombs were reported at 2 p.m. and that they therefore probably fell some two and a half to three minutes earlier. The real picture of the raid of which it was a part is probably:

13h. 57m. 30s. Thirteen bombs dropped.
13h. 57m. 45s. Five aeroplanes seen (now $1\frac{1}{4}$ miles away).

13h. 58m. 00s. Alarm given (bombers now 2½ miles away).
14h. 42m. 00s. All clear.

The maximum distance between any two bombs (marked with crosses on the map) is such that, supposing both were dropped by the same bomber, the raid could have been over in less than thirty seconds.

It will be seen therefore that our estimate of two minutes' danger per raid is generous. It will also be seen that the problems of the passive defence are very serious indeed. *Even if Barcelona were honeycombed with refuges, nobody could have got to them in this particular raid unless they had taken refuge before the raid began.* Moreover, salvage corps, ambulances, doctors are required for hundreds of victims all within thirty seconds at thirteen different spots.

That is a raid as a whole. I would ask the reader to bear in mind the relation of this reality with orthodox A.R.P. Let us now look in detail at what High Explosive does in any one instance.

54

II

The action of a High Explosive bomb consists of a rapid succession of five processes. It creates the scenes with which this report

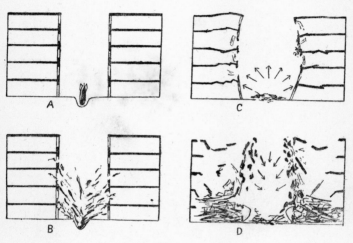

Fig. 3

is illustrated in a way that can be described diagrammatically.

Fig. 3 shows the section of a Barcelona street like those in Plate XII, with six-storied houses on each side. A bomb has dropped somewhere in this street. What happens?

(1) The bomb penetrates into the ground, forming a crater the size of which can be estimated for various weights of bombs dropping from various heights (Fig. 3A).

The chief damage done by this is to destroy pipes and wires. If the bomb falls on the roof of a house, it is able to pass through every ceiling and bury itself in the cellar floor. The damage is usually obscured by later events, but the few unexploded bombs that I have seen left a neat circular hole in each ceiling as they passed. Plate III shows the hole in the cellar enlarged by subsequent explosion of a bomb that pierced from the roof downward. It will be noted that the least destroyed part of the house even from this direct hit is the top part. This is not always so, in fact, examination of ruins suggests that it is merely a matter of chance what part of a house, if any, escapes.

In early days the streets of Barcelona were covered with posters telling how much concrete and earth were necessary to stop bombs of various heights. These have been removed.

The calculations show that a 100-kilo bomb falling from 1,000 metres requires 7.50 metres of earth or 1 metre of concrete to stop it, while one weighing 1,000 kilos requires 20 metres of earth or 2 metres of concrete. It is clear, therefore, that no building is safe from a bomb falling 1,000 metres, let alone from one falling 3,000 metres.

But the dangers from the mere penetration of the bomb are irrelevant, since the later processes are far more serious.

(2) The bomb explodes. In doing so it throws the fragments of its case in all directions, knocking pieces off buildings, killing passers-by, or people indoors if it enters at a window (Fig. 3B).

Plate XIX shows the vast clouds of dust which rise from the explosion. It hangs over the scene for hours and impedes the rescue work as in Plate XXI.

None of the damage shown in our plates is due to this explosion, except perhaps the chips in the pillar behind the figure in white in Plate XXXI. After an explosion there may be dead bodies in the street for a hundred yards and more, but very few will be due to shrapnel. Most of the bodies will not bear the mark of any wound at all. They have been killed by the processes which follow immediately after the explosion.

(3) The explosion sets the air around it into violent motion. The air expands with enormous force so that the walls of the buildings are pressed inwards against the horizontal floors and roofs. These are buckled up at lines of least resistance as in Fig. 3C. The weaker parts of the walls, e.g., the windows with their frames, are forced into the rooms as in Plate VI, where we see a bedroom floor covered with fragments of glass. It was originally hoped that by protecting glass with strips of paper (Plate V) it would be possible to conserve them; but the force of expansion is too great, the strips may protect the inmates from splinters of glass, but when the whole frame comes away in one, *it will be readily seen that dreams of 'gas-proof' rooms are dissolved.*

It is even considered advisable to *open* windows so that in the event of a bomb

58

falling not too close, those parts of the house which are weaker will not be destroyed. In the case of the bomb near the Coliseum, glass and frames were shattered at least four hundred yards away.

In the event of gas and High Explosive being used at the same time, people would have to make a choice between opening their windows to avoid the frames being pushed in and closing them in the hope that they would afford protection against gas. It would depend upon the distance that a succeeding explosion chanced to be whether they had guessed right.

(4) Immediately after the expansion the pocket of rarified air produced by it is crushed in by the whole weight of the surrounding atmosphere. This acts upon the buildings as if a force were sucking them towards the centre of the explosion (Fig. 3D). This has even more serious results than (3).

The superior destructivity of the suction is due to a number of reasons, but notably to the stresses which an architect allows for in his plans. These are all for forces like wind from outside inwards. Such forces push the front wall back against the floor joists. Now comes the suction to suck the whole front wall away from the house. It comes away like the front of a doll's house when it is unhooked, and the unsupported floors fall down into the cellar. These effects are beautifully illustrated in Plate X, where the front of the houses have been sucked into the street, carrying with them a part of the side walls. Immediately after, the floors, left without support, have plunged into the cellars. All this has been produced by the suction from one bomb.

Plate XI illustrates the effect of suction from a more distant explosion. Here the structure of the building remains standing, but the corrugated steel doors (the left-hand one is still visible) have been sucked out into the road. I have seen a whole block of more than a hundred yards in length in which every steel door on both sides has been bellied out towards the centre of the street by this effect of suction. In this case the window-frames and glass were all pushed inwards by the preceding moment of pressure. It will be readily seen that High Explosive opens the door and window to gas.

Plates XIII and XVII show a capricious effect of suction. It will be noticed that on some of the walls there still remain pictures and mirrors unbroken and virtually undisturbed. This at first sight seems odd. There is nothing so surprising as to contemplate a house almost totally wrecked and to see a few objects serenely where they should be. Thus in one house which had lost all its six floors and the whole front wall, there remained on a side wall on the third floor, exposed to view from the street, a shelf containing ten cardboard filing cases side by side and two others on top of them, all in perfect order. In another house in the poverty-stricken Fifth District, nothing remained except high up silhouetted against the sky a drying rack with unbroken crockery.

If we understand the nature of suction, we can see how such things happen. The suck-

ing force is expended on the outer surface
of the front wall. It pulls this away and as
a secondary effect the floors and ceilings it
was supporting fall also; but there never was
any force exerted against the back wall, and
so there the mirror remains, unbroken and
hanging straight.

Such pictures explain why in various
Spanish towns an effort is being made to
save historic monuments by casing them in
an outer wall, as in Plate VII. This will not
only protect the building from pieces of flying shrapnel, but, in the event of a bomb
falling near by, the force of suction will be
expended on the protecting wall, which will
be torn away in such a manner that with
any luck the real wall will be left intact.

The case of the bridge at Culera (Plate
IV) is a clear demonstration of the greater
danger from suction. The uprights of the
parapet were joined by curved walls of thin
bricks curving outwards. A bomb dropped
on the mountain-side nearly half a mile
away and sucked these walls away towards
itself.

Plate XIV very graphically illustrates the force of this air expansion and suction. The metal lamp-post has not been struck by flying fragments: it has been twisted and gnarled like a tree in a prevailing wind.

Plate XIII shows that it is not necessarily the lower floors that suffer least. The suction came from a bomb outside in the street, yet the top floor alone remains, with total wreckage beneath. Evidently the roof itself was more strongly riveted to the front wall than the lower ceilings, and the line of fracture therefore came below this floor, leaving the hanging lamp unharmed above a chasm.

In Plate XVII an accident of structure has left a small piece of the front rooms intact.

(5) A fifth effect can best be described as the accompanying earthquake. It is not so spectacular in its results, but has very important connection with the problem of what part of a building is most safe from High Explosive. The effect of an explosion is not confined to the air: it is continued through the solid ground. One obvious practical consideration resulting from (5) is

that when calculating the amount of ferro-concrete needed to safeguard a shelter, you must not only consider effect (1). It is no use the concrete stopping the penetration if the earthquake effect is going to cause the shelter to cave in, with the weight of concrete coming on the heads of the refugees.

Moreover, many a cellar which will be excellent against effect (4) will be fatal owing to effect (5).

This simple description of the complicated effects of High Explosive need not be pro-longed to describe the modifications when the bomb falls on a house rather than in the street outside. A direct hit is no more and no less dangerous than the explosion near by which sucks away the front of your house.

12

Such being the nature of High Explosive bombing, what light is thrown on orthodox A.R.P. by a study of it?

I do not propose to spend time discussing those parts of orthodox A.R.P. which are clearly inadequate, such as the provision of gas-proof rooms which will cease to be gas-proof within a wide area of any High Explosive bomb. It will suffice to glance at a Barcelona poster still considered to contain wisdom. It shows how A.R.P. folk-lore seems to have been evoked from somebody's inner consciousness and copied from one country to another; no doubt it does very well in a vacuum of ignorance until a raid comes along to blow it away with more material things.

In Fig. 4 most of the drawings contain advice which will be familiar to English readers. The advice is sensible but trivial. It can claim a psychological justification in that it is a good thing for people to have something to do so long as they are left with limbs and senses to do it.

By all means 1, put out the lights; 2, shut doors and windows (unless you belong to the opposing school of thought to which we have referred above); 3, put out fires; 4, turn off water and gas mains; 5, get your overcoat and gas mask; 6, and your tinned foods; 7, and your electric torch; 8, and if you like

E

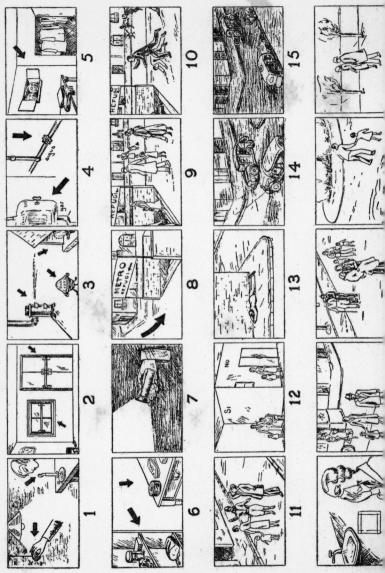

Fig. 4

terrified crowds go to your refuge even if you cannot get there in time for the bombs; 9, with dignity; 10, without hurry; 11, without staring about; all this is only plain common sense and was doubtless thought of by someone who has never seen an air-raid; but 12 is more interesting. You are advised to stand in the corner of an inner wall and not by an outer wall with a door and a window. A glance at some of our plates will show that there is something to be said for this advice. In Plates X, XIII and XVII there are fragments of floor left in such a position; and it is just conceivable that people might maintain their balance and watch the floors above and the furniture in the rest of the room disappear into the cellar.

13 is even more sensible, especially as the wall seems to have remained intact. It is certainly good advice for anyone in a street to fling himself on his face; moreover, it is the position used by some religions for prayer. I have a friend who says he escaped thus from a very small bomb that exploded five yards from him. That one should leave

67

one's car properly parked is good advice and the damp handkerchief has its points, although the fourth picture may make it hard to turn on the tap at this late hour. 17, get out of the tram; 18, help children, aged and paralytics—unexceptionable advice; and finally flee damp spots and walk against the wind! All governments produce this sort of thing. Perhaps it is intended as part of a faith cure.

Nevertheless, A.R.P. is a science as well as a faith, even in the light of the very unpleasant facts that we have been considering, and I propose to deal with a few of the vital points where practical steps are possible.

13

The fundamental error in most A.R.P. planning is that the city is regarded as made up of individuals who can be allowed to remain without working for a long time in conditions as near safety as possible.

But if the Attack brings London to a standstill then the Attack has won the war. Protection we must have, but only within limits which make it possible also for the city to keep moving. The Attack hopes to keep the city from moving, both materially by tying up traffic amid destroyed thoroughfares and psychologically by tying up human nerves so that men do not know where to go. *It cannot be too much emphasized that in ideal circumstances, with a bomb-proof shelter for everyone, the Defence will still lose the war, perhaps without suffering a casualty, if everyone sits in a shelter and does nothing for long enough on end.* Therefore:

A.R.P. MUST PROVIDE FOR INDIVIDUAL SAFETY AND AT THE SAME TIME COMMUNAL ACTIVITY.

By communal activity we mean something far wider than the mere keeping of streets open to traffic. Yet this comparatively straightforward problem is all that our Home Office memoranda have so far considered. We will deal with the minor question first and then discuss the maintenance of 'communal activity' in the wider sense.

The British Home Office have issued A.R.P. memorandum No. 2, "Rescue Parties and Clearance of Debris," in which the problem is described as follows:

"It would be of vital importance . . . that roads should be kept open to traffic, and that, if many roads were damaged, those which were of greater traffic value should be first repaired. . . .

"The clearance of the obstruction in roads should not present serious problems in the matter of labour. . . .

"But the organization for directing the work needs careful forethought. . . .

"The need for reopening the road for the passage of vehicles might conceivably be so urgent that some part of it would have to be levelled immediately—e.g., by the use of debris from neighbouring buildings."

(*In passing, it is interesting to glance at Plates XXII and XXIII. In most cases the suction deposits a great deal more debris into the road than is required to fill holes. We must be prepared to remove mountains rather than to level roads.)

"Where damage to roads was accompanied by gas contamination, the services of the decontaminating squad would be required in the first instance; but apart from that contingency the work of the highway authority would be work which would be carried out by its ordinary employees. . . . All regular employees should therefore be trained in anti-gas precautions."

Actual rescue of bodies from buildings is to be carried out by rescue parties of two sorts, 'heavy' with eight men and 'light' with six men. If we look at Plates XXII and XXIII we see the sort of job that these squads will have to carry out.

The street is a very narrow one-way street situated in the centre of the lower margin of Plate 8-9. The time taken to clear it was something like two weeks. Admittedly the street was unimportant from the point of view of traffic and, but for the need of rescuing the buried casualties, it might have been left indefinitely. But if Chancery Lane were to be blocked as completely it would be important to clear it.

The time taken was over two weeks. For the first few days clearance must be very slow indeed as the debris must be moved by the handful. There can be no mechanical shovels so long as people may be underneath. Plate XXIV shows the only practicable technique. Through the half-open doorway we see the debris of several floors fallen to the ground. The victims are below this in the basement, and the helpers are removing material by hand in the hopes of freeing them without further injury.

Plate XXVI illustrates the same problem when the debris is in the street. Plates XXV and XXVII show very plainly why the process must be slow. Two victims have been released from under the heavy blocks of fallen masonry, and mechanical appliances would probably have destroyed them. There is a significant detail in Plate XXV. The rules insist that rescue work must begin at the first moment after the explosion has been reported and that not only the trained squads but all able-bodied neighbours should help. The work must go on, moreover, even if another raid begins. We can see in the faces of the two men in the foreground that this is happening at the moment the photo was taken.

An eyewitness account will make some of the problems of road clearance more vivid for us: "On Saturday, March 19th, I paid a visit to Calle Arimon, where a six-storied block of flats had been destroyed. The street is narrow and about fifty yards from end to end. It was entirely blocked and impassable to traffic.

"Twenty-four hours after the bombing many bodies had not yet been recovered. Two armed members of the Guardia de Asalto were on duty at either end of the street. They stopped all male passers-by to find men able to help in the work. The production of one's documentation was necessary to prove that one was already engaged on work of importance.

"As the heart of the city had for three days previously been subjected to continuous bombardment from the air it was not easy to find man-power.

"Engaged in the work at this spot were some dozen boys of the Boy Scout age. Most were lined up chain fashion and passed on from hand to hand bricks, masonry, pieces of furniture, etc. Others were poking about with sticks trying to locate the bodies of their parents and brothers and sisters. One solitary guard was assisting.

"A boy suddenly called a halt by a shout that he had found something. The guard went quickly to the spot and lifted out the body of a child of two or three.

"It was entirely naked as the force of the explosion had burnt away every shred of clothing. The Guard looked at it closely for a moment and in a flash recognized it as his own child.

"He wrapped the remains in some linen from the pile and signalled to the workers to continue. The other Guard went to telephone to the mortuary."

It will be noted that the work was made more difficult by the lack of personnel. The trained organized groups were engaged on more vital tasks. Our Home Office contemplates a need for "six parties of six or eight men for every 100,000 population in urban areas." This seems an underestimate of probable needs. It allows 700 men for Barcelona. If it took 100 men 24 hours a day two weeks to clear one bomb out of 200 fallen within 40 hours, where would Barcelona traffic be even now on our Home Office ration?

There is a vital difference between the problem of personnel in Barcelona and the same problem as it is envisaged by our authorities.

The latter contemplate the recruitment by voluntary means of semi-skilled labourers to clear away the debris. It is probably not thought likely that should a bomb drop in Park Lane the uninjured guests of the Dorchester Hotel will be expected to help pick their hotel out of the middle of the road. But it is doubtful if the problem can really be solved on the basis of professionalism. In Barcelona the fall of a bomb is regarded as the concern of all the neighbours. They have already organized to elect their own

75

air-raid wardens and have worked out a technique for dealing with events as they happen. When a siren gives a warning they have house representatives who get the inhabitants to whatever shelter has been decided on. In early days quite an elaborate system of moving people to the lower floors was in vogue, but experience has proved this to be futile. But the 'responsable' ushers people to the best places, counts them, helps them and keeps up their morale. If a bomb falls he goes at once to telephone the authorities and then collects all the available neighbours to do whatever is needed. Every able-bodied survivor turns to, under the direction of the technicians, to do what he can.

Naturally the advantages and disadvantages of the British class system of civilization will make themselves felt in a future air raid, but one may be permitted to observe, even in a technical discussion, that the practical problems of A.R.P. cannot be solved by telephoning for some workmen to come and clear away the mess outside the front door.

Certain social divisions which are second nature in England in time of peace will be eliminated by the force of high explosive.

If we turn now to the bomb which caused so much damage in the Corts we have an even more significant illustration of our problem. The Corts is a wide main artery; it took six days to reach the last entombed victim and two weeks to open the road to full traffic. An average of one hundred men were kept working night and day to achieve this result.

If we look at the map of Barcelona we see that the conditions in the Corts are not unlike what would happen if a bomb fell in Piccadilly Circus near the Café Royal. Such a bomb would deposit most of the Piccadilly Hotel and the buildings opposite into the street. Effect 1 (see p. 56) would damage the steel drum supporting the Circus over the tube station. Effect 2 would kill passers-by in Regent Street, the Circus, Piccadilly, Lower Regent Street, Shaftesbury Avenue. Effect 3 would blow in every window-frame and doorway within two hundred yards.

Effect 4 would deposit the fronts of all buildings for at least one hundred yards into the streets, and Effect 5 would disturb the tube station and escalators beneath the surface. Apart from deaths and material damage the bomb would block at least three main thoroughfares with debris sown with corpses and injured sufferers. In no circumstances could mechanical appliances be used for several days, however important it might be to open up traffic. The map of Barcelona makes very clear by contrast with a map of London how much easier is the task of keeping that well-planned city open to transport.

It must be accepted as an axiom that London could not be kept clear in war time for the normal traffic of peace time.

A.R.P. planners must begin by realizing that only a radical alteration of the habits of a city can make possible the continued efficiency of the city in war time. The problem is not to teach the city to wait in safety while the raiders roll by but to devise a city that can still function in spite of raiders.

It is not the people who must go underground to wait: it is the movement of the city that must go underground. High Explosive will dislocate surface traffic to a serious degree, and all plans must be made now to reply to this strong point of the Attack.

In short it is the duty of A.R.P. planners to counteract the difficulties that will be put in the way of surface traffic:

1. By eliminating irrelevant traffic
    (*a*) those who are not needed to carry out the work of war must be evacuated to keep the streets clear of them.
    (*b*) those who are needed must change their habits, e.g., they will have to sleep where they work; there will be no room for diurnal migration to and from the suburbs.
2. By extending facilities for underground traffic.

To these points we shall return later. They are the least of the difficulties presented by High Explosive. If we can keep men's nerves capable of reasonable action we can certainly devise a material environment in which they can act. But can we do this? It will be best to defer consideration of material planning until we have set out more fully the psychological problem that must first be solved. Then only can we realize the extent and nature of the problem of safeguarding 'communal activity.'

PART III

PANIC

14

THE Technique of Silent Approach combined with High Explosive bombs as used by the Italo-Germans in their March Barcelona manœuvres is not intended to attack military objectives; it is not intended to cause crippling casualties: it is directed against the nerves of the people.

A modern State at war depends for its strength on two main factors, men at the front working like parts of a machine, and a population at the rear working like rational human beings. The technique of smashing the machine is quite different from the technique of preventing the population from continuing to work like rational human beings.

If men have been trained to the perfect performance of mechanical action they have to be physically smashed in order to dislocate them. Artillery and aircraft must pound them and score direct hits. This technique is wasteful, inconvenient and therefore useless for preventing the civilian population from working like rational beings. They can best be immobilized—that is irrationalized—by suspense. There is no need to smash them physically; instead they must be dislocated psychologically, and then they become actually more useful to the enemy alive than dead.

The Technique of Silent Approach combined with High Explosive is the most admirable achievement of the modern art of war for the performance of this psychological task.

The beginning of all A.R.P. wisdom consists in realizing that the Defence is faced with a psychological danger. The Attack has devised a weapon which can stop the population from functioning like rational human beings. The Defence must maintain the rationality and the activity of its population or be defeated. Any A.R.P. pro-

gramme that does not secure both rationality and activity is futile.

I have been at some pains to discover how
people actually behaved in Barcelona under
the stresses set up by Silent Approach.
It is not easy; active forgetting is very
much in evidence. You might as well
question a recovered mental patient as to
the content of his hallucinations during an
attack as ask the average Barcelona man
what happened during those forty hours.
Those who had something active to do could
tell you what they did, but the passive sufferers have lost all sense of time, sequence,
or detail.

I was able to learn the facts of the raids
from the official and very accurate log of
the Junta de Defensa Passiva, and I noted
that whenever I was able to check a story
of personal experience against these scienti-
fically recorded facts the story was always
grossly inaccurate.

Certain generally held but nevertheless
quite inaccurate beliefs may be mentioned.
First, everyone was certain that 'thousands

of bombs' fell. A cool analysis of the facts
suggests that the total number did not ex-
ceed two hundred, including those in the
suburbs.

*It may be taken as axiomatic that the
population will always confuse bombs and
anti-aircraft fire and be as affected by one
as by the other, unless special pains are
taken to help them.*

I have already referred to the universal
belief that the bombs were 'liquid air' bombs.
This belief is held by thousands who had
never heard of liquid air and cannot know
what it is. The basis of the belief is that the
effect of the explosive was considered to be
worse in these raids than in others. Except
for the damage at the Coliseum I was unable to find evidence that this was so. What
made the bombs seem worse was the technique in conjunction with which they were
used. It was Silent Approach repeated
again and again that heightened the effect
on the people's nerves. Everybody believed that they were in the centre of the
worst part of the raids. One cool and

experienced observer admitted that "when they began to drop all round here I couldn't stick it any longer and went up to such and such a place." Actually no bomb dropped within a mile of him, and when he retired he went nearer to the place where the nearest bomb had dropped.

I propose to deal with the evidence in so far as it helps to provide a psychological basis for reasonable A.R.P.

15

There are four psycho-physiological facts, commonplaces to all who study human behaviour, which are vitally connected with the problem of devising a defence against the Technique of Silent Approach combined with High Explosive.

1. Noise can act physiologically like a chemical poison. It has been shown that sudden noise produces rapid changes in blood pressure so considerable that in time the circulatory system deteriorates, while a normal nervous balance is immediately

than the prick itself. It follows that it is not necessary to prick a person all the time to produce emotional chaos. It is better, easier, and cheaper to keep him in suspense expecting a prick.

The Technique of Silent Approach is the Attack's best method of creating mental chaos through suspense. The Defence has to counter this in some way or other, and we may say in passing that *one of the chief faults in orthodox A.R.P. is that far from these being designed to minimize suspense and strain they very often play into the hands of the Attack by increasing it.*

3. If a large crowd of people is gathered together in conditions of unpleasant stimulus plus growing suspense the deleterious effects on individuals are increased and spread like an infection to others.

In such a crowd emotions are magnified and reasonableness cancelled out. The crowd as a whole becomes as irrational as its least rational members. There is an exception to this rule: if the crowd is knit together to perform a common rational activity it may be more useful than any of its members. If the crowd is doing nothing, it will more easily succumb to irrational activity, that is to panic. If the crowd is doing something it may be a source of strength to its individual members even in the face of unpleasant stimuli. In short, *if there must be a crowd under difficult circumstances it should be a working crowd, not a waiting crowd. This should be a fundamental axiom for all A.R.P.*

4. If the dislocating stimuli are repeated there will come a time when the individuals subjected to them will cease to function on the rational plane. They will regress to a condition of meaningless, useless and therefore dangerous action. It is not that they will be afraid. The demoralization does not consist in an intelligent striving after safety —if that were usual, air raids would not be so successful—it consists in a reversion to a pre-rational condition of fatuous motor reaction, and this leads to panic.

If we consider the implications of these psycho-physiological facts we may establish A.R.P. on a reasonable basis. If they are ignored, A.R.P. must fail. The Attack has set a problem; it is no use for the Defence to busy itself with some quite different problem. The Technique of Silent Approach with High Explosive must be dealt with psychologically since it amounts to the creating of a tremendously powerful attack on the enemy's nerve centres.

If there is an air raid on London it is very unlikely that military objectives will be hit except by chance. Indeed, to withdraw one single bomber from attacking military objectives at the Front so that it may hit them in London would amount to criminal negligence on the part of any High Command guilty of it.

If there is an air raid on London only a very few people will be killed, say ten or fifteen thousand, in a week of raids, a very expensive way of reducing the Defence's man-power, especially seeing that many of the victims would be women and children, who can be turned into a greater asset by the Attack if they are kept alive.

If there is an air raid on London the material damage will be relatively small and unjustifiable from the point of view of military science except, as we have seen, in so far as transport and movement can be tied up as a result. An enemy which wasted time and forces destroying Buckingham Palace instead of pounding a few hundred square yards of front-line trenches would be as incompetent as a duellist who aimed at his opponent's ear rather than at his heart.

But if there is an air raid on London its object will be to produce panic. *It will be a race between the Attack trying to create panic and the Defence trying to prevent panic.* Active Defence will try to foil the Attack by new counter-methods and by attrition. It will succeed so long as Passive Defence is so organized that it can delay the onset of panic long enough. It is to Barcelona that A.R.P. should be looking for light on this fundamental problem.

16

Consider the time-table on page 33. By designing it the Attack has created an ideal psychological weapon. It dislocates the habits of a huge population. It tangles the web of social thought and action inextricably. If we add a few more hours to the time-table, hours which must have been filled with growing suspense seeing that nobody knew that the ordeal was over, we have a remarkable forty-eight hours of mental stress.

To be healthy and normal most human beings must spend their forty-eight hours in conformity with such a pattern as this:

Two periods of eight hours' sleep,
Two periods of eight hours' work,
Four periods of rest and recreation.

Silent Approach with High Explosive turns this into:

Thirteen two-minute periods of danger and terror,
Nine hours or so of fear without danger,
Thirty-six hours of growing suspense.

There can be no doubt as to the results. To begin with nobody slept during two nights, and a city from which sleep has been banished for 48 hours is a city on its way to disintegration.

But the effect was no mere banishing of sleep. Waking consciousness passed into a hypnogogic state. "That night also I could not sleep. The memory of what I had seen overtaxed my senses. For some days I lived in a bad dream.

"That house wide open from top to bottom, leaving all its intimate family details exposed . . . I shall always be seeing it."

This eyewitness is typical in that he speaks not of the danger but of a hideous incongruity. Another man, as emotionally tough as could be wished—he tried to blow up King Alfonso while still in his teens—said : "It was horrible; I cannot describe it; you would have to have seen it to understand; why, at four hundred metres from the explosion I saw men walking who were absolutely white to their eyelashes, covered in dust from the destroyed buildings; I cannot describe how it made me feel."

A girl who still wore her ankle bandaged from a wound wrote: "When the Red Cross came they put me in a car to take me home. On the way it was horrible, whole houses down. On the ground I saw white sheets covered with blood. They were sheets people put over corpses. It was horrible. Now, two months after, I cannot remember clearly what I did see." It is as if the mind concentrated its scanty power of memory over one concrete detail, a detail which no doubt had a special significance for the psychological history of the individual.

"The same day," said another, "two hours earlier, a bomb fell near a tram. My woman-janitor was on the platform. The arm and shoulder of a youth was severed by the explosion, and his body dropped at her feet. She pushed it away and sprang from the tram and ran away. She was caught and taken to hospital. To this day she cries whenever she hears sirens or even when a motor-horn having a similar noise is sounded. Before she was a healthy woman of the peasant type of constitution."

A stenographer wounded in the raids: "Even to-day I have a confused picture of what I saw; I can only remember a lot of dead women and children."

My general impression after talking to a great many people is that a consciousness of personal danger from the bombs was never their uppermost feeling or memory. It would seem that they were pounded into a dazed condition by the experience, and most of all by the noise, and that having reached that condition some one exterior detail, not directly concerning their own comfort or safety, but doubtless linking up with some significant episode of their past emotional history took complete possession of their mind. Thus the experience of those hours of repeated raids becomes condensed for one individual into a memory of stained sheets, for another of figures white with dust, for a third of the incongruous intimacies exposed when the front of a house disappears.

Everywhere of course active forgetting was to be observed. I spoke to a boy of fourteen who had been pinned under some wreckage side by side with his mother's corpse. I asked him what he remembered. He replied: "Nothing at all," but as he said it, it was clear from the spasmodic movements of his hands that they 'remembered.' He had no idea whether he had been buried for an hour or a day, but the traumatic shock and repression will be with him permanently.

17

The Attack has created this tremendous psychological danger; what can the Defence do to neutralize it? There will be a tendency in some quarters to sidetrack the whole problem by pointing out the immense difficulty of adapting the Technique of Silent Approach to London. We may readily agree that the Defence will be better prepared and that the problem is more difficult for the Attack; but, even admitting this, it is essential to realize that the potency of this Technique, the devastating effect on the

Defence when it is successful, are such that the Attack will continue to improve its methods so as to outdistance the Defence's counter-measures. The Defence must at least insist on A.R.P. that give it the maximum time to devise better and better active measures, such as new detectors, larger patrol fleets, more deadly anti-aircraft barrages. In short, A.R.P. must stave off the moment of panic as long as possible.

Let us begin with the problem of noise. The earlier raids on Barcelona were not very noisy. I had the impression that the better morale, the greater indifference that the Barcelona public seemed to show compared with what I remembered of the London public in the Great War was at least partly due to this.

Later impressions have confirmed this. In London it was the noise that created fear. In Barcelona at first, owing to the pact of non-intervention, there were scarcely any anti-aircraft guns. Now that there are perhaps a score of them the danger to morale from noise is increased. "The bombs are

G

of course terrible," one friend told me, "but it is the anti-aircraft guns that frighten people most. They go on and on, and people think they are bombs." The Defence must realize that the anti-aircraft barrage is a two-edged weapon. If it inconveniences the Attack, well and good, but it puts a strain on the Defence by reason of the psychological effect of its noise. Anyone who can remember London in war time remembers conversations like this: "Just listen to that." "That's only the anti-aircraft guns." "Oh, is it? Thank goodness." This is of course perfectly irrational, since any noise can only tell of past danger; but it must be borne in mind. Every effort should be made to help the public to distinguish between 'them,' i.e., the bombs which are no longer dangerous because they have fallen, and 'us,' i.e., our anti-aircraft guns which are driving the danger away.

A.R.P. that pay attention to psychological problems will include the mechanism needed to ensure this. Instead of leaving the public in the dark, precisely the same commentator system which the B.B.C. uses for cricket matches or naval reviews can be adapted to this task. In every place where crowds are likely to assemble, in every shelter, in every office and home, the voice of the B.B.C. commentator should be heard: "The bombers have already dropped their bombs; you are therefore safe; the noise you hear is our own barrage driving the raiders away; keep cool and stop where you are; the danger is over; no bombs are falling; the danger is now over; our barrage is dealing with the enemy; everybody here has been behaving splendidly; the morale is perfect; stop where you are till the 'all-clear' sounds; but remember the danger is over."

We should realize that if the public confuses all sounds and imagines them equally to be bombs, its picture of the forces arrayed against it is grossly magnified; to counter this it must be given a chance to identify itself with the noise, to see it as 'our' noise, 'my' noise, something I am doing to defeat the enemy. The whole city then sees itself as hitting back at a few intrepid scoundrels;

a far more healthy psychological attitude than any possible if bombs and anti-aircraft are confused.

It is even debatable whether anti-aircraft should be used as often and in the places where it is at present contemplated. Our technicians cannot judge of the value of the barrage unless they are prepared to bear in mind the psychological disadvantages of the noise.

What can the barrage do when it is opposed with Silent Approach? The argument that, although the barrage does not hit them, it keeps them high is fallacious. When the Attack deliberately adopts Silent Approach it does not need to be kept high, and, moreover, the barrage cannot keep the raiders out of the ring. Nobody is likely to contemplate a permanent barrage from the moment war begins, and the barrage is useless once the bombs have been dropped. It is possible that the military faith in barrage against raiders dates from the day when it was assumed that the object of the raid would be to attack military objectives; now that it is

morale that is attacked, since morale can
be as well attacked from ten thousand feet
as from one thousand, many of the argu-
ments for barrage are obsolete. But the
danger from the barrage's noise is not in
any way obsolete.

The most that the barrage can do is with
a great deal of luck to destroy a few bombers
on their return journey, and against this
must be put the damage done to the Defence's nerves by noise.

It would of course be nonsense to advo-
cate the abolition of the barrage altogether.
It must be there to counteract other air-raid
techniques. What I am suggesting is that
when the Technique of Silent Approach has
been successful and the bombers, having
dropped their loads, are in full flight, the barrage does no good compared with the appalling harm done by its noise.

The noise of the High Explosive bombs
is naturally not in the power of the Defence
to stop. Nothing can alleviate its horror
at close quarters. Many people tried to

describe the noise of the 'new' High Explosive bombs, the 'liquid air' bombs as they insisted on calling them. This noise is 'far more frightening,' it is 'worse,' 'quite different'; it 'seems to be somehow deeper or more profound'; it is 'not a noise really.' Without suggesting that gas masks are going to be quite useless it is at least possible to suggest that ear protectors and sound deadeners will be as useful. It is more than probable that the noise of High Explosive will always be more valuable to the Attack than gas.

The third form of noise created by air-raid warfare is entirely in the hands of the Defence, and moreover it is controlled by the A.R.P. authorities themselves without interference from military commands.

It is the air-raid warning, for the misuse of which there can be no excuse. But so long as psychological considerations are ignored the air-raid warning will be a source of danger to the Defence.

First of all there is the nature of the noise. The siren is the usual form chosen, and solely because a siren can produce noise more economically than any other mechanical contrivance.

"It is the peculiar sound of the siren that frightens me," I was told by one man. "It is like something chasing you down the street."

There can be no doubt that the siren is emotionally disturbing. Many people have observed that a fog-horn on board ship affects them 'out of all proportion.' So with the siren; it is a direct attack on the nerves; it is a 'moaning' and a 'wailing,' a frightening thing in itself; an additional source of fear; it should not be used. *The fundamental thing that must be realized is that we do not want a warning of danger; we want a call to action. We do not want to frighten people; we want to make them answer or call to act in pursuit of their own safety.*

Better than a siren would be a few sharp musical notes associated in everybody's mind with useful action, a bugle call or a snatch of a popular melody. Anything at least but the paralysing 'weirdness' of a siren. And the best solution would once more be an adaptation of the technique of the B.B.C. commentator: "Please take shelter. Please take shelter. You have plenty of time. Keep cool and take shelter."

In the second place great care must be taken as to when the air-raid warning should be used. In Barcelona the siren sounds even when the Technique of Silent Approach has been successful and the bombs have already dropped. This is playing into the hands of the Attack.

No air-raid signal should ever be given unless it can be heard in time for useful action to be taken in obedience to it. Directly it is realized that the signal should not be a warning of danger—especially of a danger which is over or so imminent as to be unavoidable—but a command to act, the folly of using it when there is no time for action becomes apparent.

Whenever the Technique of Silent Approach has failed and the Defence has spotted the attackers at least a minute before they can reach their target, then the signal should be given, but never otherwise; for any air-raid warning, being of its nature the creator of suspense, must work psychologically in favour of the Attack; its use must therefore be avoided by the Defence unless the advantages outweigh this very real disadvantage.

The problem of noise from the point of view of the Defence may be summed up thus: noise as noise is productive of anxiety; it can best be sterilized by attaching to it a suitable and reassuring idea; to the noise of the High Explosive bomb the idea 'the danger from that is over'; to the barrage, 'that is our reply to them; that is ourselves acting,' and to the warning, 'we must act.'

Above all we must combat the noise of High Explosive, since we cannot control it; and it is very fortunate that the idea that 'the danger is past' is no mere faith cure but the truth. The more we can associate all noise with past danger the better, which makes it all the more necessary to be careful how we use noises for alarms of future or present danger.

18

We pass from the problem of noise to the more general problem of suspense. When will the rain begin? When will the next bomb fall? When will they come back? These are the questions which breed the uncontrollable form of anxiety which is the first stage of panic.

A.R.P. must aim at reducing the amount of suspense felt by each member of the civilian population. There is one fundamental rule to be observed; suspense is the cumulative effect of alarm followed by inactivity.

I was able to observe the behaviour of various people in an office during a raid in Barcelona during the last week of May, 1938. It was the first raid I had seen since the March raids so completely altered the natural human reactions to air attack.

Before March, as I have said, people erred in the direction of too little caution. A raid was something to look at. Now all was changed. Everybody round me had been through the terrifying experiences of those days. There were people working and people waiting; the two groups behaved quite differently.

The people waiting at once began to display those motor reflexes which show that a mental system under strain is reverting to primitive unco-ordinated movements in order to relieve the strain by action. Some were pale and still; others walked about rapidly; two women were sick; one or two looked about them at their companions with that inquiring look which denotes that the individual feels out of his depth and is looking for a lead from outside. On the other hand the people working continued to work for a minute or two and then stopped and went to the window and looked out. In the streets which had only partially cleared the men were walking with a quickened pace, but the women in several instances seemed to be brought to a standstill and to be undecided as to where they should go. In none of these groups was there any sign that the altered behaviour pattern was conducive to any useful action. The people who were working bore up better than the ones who were waiting, but I had the impression that 'business as usual' was an antidote for fear for at best a very short time.

A.R.P. must not expect any good results from people waiting or even from people trying to carry on as if nothing was happening. A.R.P. must first realize that waiting is fatal and that action is essential, and second that this action must be artificial and arranged to counteract an abnormal strain. Under this strain those who have work to do seek a refuge in that work, and those who have no work are forced back to the level of infantile and useless reflexes which are the first step towards panic. Once more we see that A.R.P. must reconstruct the life of the community to meet the new strains, rather than be satisfied with certain 'safety' measures of an architectural and engineering nature.

Take for example the life to be led in a gas-proof room. (Assuming that gas-proof rooms are still seriously considered.) The

Home Office memoranda advise books. This is only a partial solution. The full solution demands that the air-raid warning be a trigger to touch off every individual to helpful activity.

One of the most dangerous results of an air raid is the sense of helplessness that it gives to any waiting person. It is not merely that the individual feels helpless to save himself—I must repeat that consciousness of personal danger does not seem very great—it is much more a realization that the ability to take a part in the communal life has vanished. Anything that will help people to feel that they are still of use, that is, that others still need them, has a steadying effect.

This is illustrated by a few words of a girl of eleven who was at school when a bomb dropped very near and partially wrecked the school building: "We were all working and listening and writing. I saw the teacher stop. There was a raid. I took my little girl friend by the hand to go down to the first floor, when a terrible wind, followed by an awful noise, knocked us over. I lost consciousness but woke up at once and found myself covered with glass, wood and dust. All my companions cried, and I cried too, but I was able to comfort my two little girl friends. We waited for our mothers to come, and each time anyone came in I was sure it was one of my family. At last my brother came, and I hung on to his neck and kissed and kissed him."

The normal emotional atmosphere of a raid is therefore a heightened reaction towards other people plus a terrible sense of futility. The strain can be lessened by giving everyone useful work as a release both of motor energy and of the pent-up desire for reassurance as to one's value to the community.

Everybody should have his appointed task in an air raid, and the task should not be one normal to their everyday life, unless the normal task is essential. Thus one individual should train himself to regard the beginning of an air raid as a signal to start making bandages and dressings; another to prepare food and drink for the rescue squads who will soon be going out on their work; people might inscribe their names in a competition to see who could get most work done during raid alarms; and, if the work could be something specifically of value for the Defence against air raids, then the competition would combine admirably several necessary emotional outlets. The competitors would have an outlet for their desire to help the Defence against the cause of their anxiety, an outlet for the competitive relationship which is part of all normal social life and an outlet for the need for motor relief of nervous strain. Instead of sweating, blushing, vomiting, fainting and acting in even more seriously futile ways they would be preparing aids for rescue squads; instead of a sense of isolation from the herd they would know that others unseen by them and like them temporarily isolated were performing the same useful tasks in common with them, all helping together to ward off the danger; instead of being left with all their normal outlets for 'friendly rivalry' blocked, 'friendly rivalry'—that highly complicated psychological entity—would be continued in new forms.

What the Attack has succeeded in doing is to break down temporarily all those complicated ramifications whereby we achieve personal satisfaction of individual problems from social contacts. The individual is like a piece of a jigsaw puzzle made of rubber. It has to find a space of more or less the right shape, though it is able to do a bit of squeezing when it finds that no space is a perfect fit. We have all squeezed ourselves into a fairly good hole, and we are more or less contented. Because we owe our content to the existence of the jigsaw puzzle as a whole we are attached to it by strong ties. Then comes the air raid and upsets our puzzle. Unless it can be put together again in some coherent form, unless we can feel that it exists, and unless we feel that we have found a new hole in the new arrangement we suffer from anxiety, suspense, panic.

The Defence has got to find means of making every individual feel that the jigsaw puzzle still exists and that he has found a hole into which he can fit. This is the first problem, and only after it is realized, only as part of its solution, should A.R.P. busy itself with cement shelters, zigzag trenches, gas-proof rooms. If these objects save life —good, but only good if they also reconstruct as rapidly as possible the social outlets without which the individual is left stranded in a welter of unsatisfied psychological needs.

An admirable example of this type of work is to be seen in Barcelona in the Blood Transfusion Service. Probably the Service was designed in the first instance simply to supply the large quantities of blood needed in Barcelona to-day, but it has produced other benefits beside blood. I watched a queue of some sixty or seventy people of all types waiting their turn to be examined and indexed for future use. It was easy to observe the sense of emotional satisfaction enjoyed by the donors. The organizing of the service has been designed with excellent appreciation of psychological verities. Every

H

political or industrial group, trades union, party, club, etc., has a Blood Service delegate who enrols donors from among the membership. These go up to the clinic and are indexed. When a sudden need comes—an air raid or a big offensive, a few minutes on the telephone mobilized a hundred, five hundred, a thousand donors through these delegates.

The donors are given a variety of motives to induce them to offer themselves; they come as representatives of their own special group; they come to help their brothers and husbands; they come because some of the neighbours were hit by the bomb that missed their house; they are also given more immediately selfish inducements. Each gets a standard breakfast after the donation, and cards enabling them to buy certain rations of food for a period; and of course they have their badges. In this way blood is acquired, but also some eight to nine thousand people never lose a sense of attachment to the community during the air raids. The number of blood donors on Dr. Duran's list is about the same as the number of people that can be housed in absolutely safe bomb-proof shelters; of the two groups I believe that the donors are most likely to come through an air raid unscathed. I believe that they are a sample of the type of crowd to be created by the Defence in order to solve the serious problem set by the Attack. It would be advisable to establish in England a similar Blood Transfusion Service immediately, not only as a surgical necessity but because it would have excellent psychological repercussions.

To sum up: Silent Approach plus High Explosive is the most powerful producer of suspense leading to panic; the Defence must counter by constructing new social outlets for those temporarily blocked by the break-down of normal social living.

19

We come now to the problem of crowds and its relation to A.R.P.

The Attack destroys some normal crowds, and the Defence as part of its countermeasures creates new and abnormal crowds. What general rules should be borne in mind in the process?

First, *we must remember the deleterious effect of any waiting crowd and the necessity therefore of turning any unavoidable crowd into a working crowd.*

Second, there is room for disagreement as to how far the creation of any crowd at all is wise, provided it can be avoided.

In the only theoretical paper that has yet appeared dealing with air-raid precautions from the psychological point of view* Dr. John Rickman has given important theoretical reasons for suggesting that the 'stay-at-home-in-a-gas-proof-room' policy is psychologically inadequate:

"The stay-at-home policy . . . does not, however, take into account the degree of aptitude for, and satisfaction from, manipulative activity (this varies greatly); it omits consideration of the mental state of persons with a claustrophobic tendency (the number of whom is many times greater than of those

*Rickman: *Lancet*, June 4th, 1938, p. 1291.

with manifest claustrophobia), and above all it does not take into consideration the fact that many find their group feelings roused more deeply and more readily in the company of their own sex, or in a society based on community of work or social interests.

"The chief objection to the stay-at-home policy . . . is that the Government does not appear in this policy as an active partner."

This is very important reasoning for the creation of crowds of some sort, but I do not think that it follows, as those who criticize the Government from another angle may suggest—that the solution is a policy of providing bomb-proof public shelters for all.

Indeed, Dr. Rickman is careful to emphasize that the weakness of the stay-at-home policy is that it does not satisfy three definite needs. It is quite clear that these needs are not satisfied any better by the promiscuous bundling of people into a shelter with nothing to do there except to wait.

Here are two accounts of typical experiences in Barcelona. First, the 'responsable' of one of the shelters speaks: "Look here," he said, "a raid's a very different matter if you see it from your house or from a refuge. Before I became a 'responsable' for this refuge I did not realize that. I only knew my own feelings, and I must say they weren't very much one way or the other. But now, *now* I can talk not only of how I feel but of how other people generally are affected.

"About five hundred come into my refuge, mostly women, old people and children. Many of them, terrified by the explosions, won't leave again for hours. Sometimes a family comes in and at once misses one of the children. Nobody knows where it is. In the dark street outside you can hear people shouting anxiously, trying to find their way. It's my habit to stand at the door with an electric torch, like a sort of lighthouse. From below me in the refuge I hear children crying, everyone complaining.

"There's plenty of misfortunes to see. There's a family, for instance, with a twenty-year-old son who's a paralytic. Every time they hear the mournful siren the father and mother, helped by the neighbours, lower him to the bottom of the refuge in a chair.

"On March 17th, at eleven o'clock at night, a family missed a child of two. The whole sky was red with explosions. The father climbed out into the street. We waited for him hour after hour. He never came back. Next day we found him in the morgue."

Another eyewitness: "I tried to go into the Metro. But that was terrible. So many people had gone there that there was no room for anyone to sit down or lie down. They stood wedged there hour after hour. Imagine children crying, with the bodies of older people stifling them; and not only the children—women got hysterical. And the smell; people urinating and defæcating as they stood, because there was nothing else they could do. It went on like that all those days."

In considering these scenes we should remember that, since the Italo-Germans used Silent Approach, the paralytic was never lowered down until after the danger was over; and that, though the crowds suffered thus for forty hours and more, the probable total time of the raids was twenty-six minutes.

A careful study of the air-raid shelter situation in Barcelona suggests the following conclusions:

1. There are perhaps eight or ten large bomb-proof shelters in a usable condition, and these are capable of housing about eight thousand of the general public.

There are also about twelve hundred private shelters belonging to large flats, government offices, etc. These are more or less safe, being mostly cellars with strengthened roofs. To many of them passers-by may go, as the law requires that all street doors be left open during a raid. There are also in the suburbs caves and tunnels dug out of hillsides which offer permanent safety with a minimum of comfort to a few hundred families who have become cave-dwellers for the duration.

There is the Metro. The three underground railways have about a score of

stations between them, and of these rather
more than half are useful as temporary
shelters. There are mysterious rumours of
great underground tunnels. It is true that
two sections of underground lines have been
excavated but never used for transport. It
is rumoured that they are used as munition
dumps. It is certain that they are not used
for refuges.

2. Perhaps 15,000 people can get to absolutely safe shelter if it should happen that
Silent Approach breaks down, and 50,000
more to reasonably safe shelter. Those who
crowd to the less safe underground stations
go to a death trap. Let us say that ten thousand out of one and a half million people were
killed and seriously wounded in the March
raids; that is one in 150 of the population.
Suppose the same proportion of the 65,000
adequately sheltered would have been casualties had they remained at home or in the
shelter of the building they were passing.
That would have been another 500 casualties. Actually the number would have been
less, since, as must always happen with

Silent Approach, only those who remained in shelter from one raid to another increased their margin of safety. And many on their own admission simply 'panicked' to shelter when they heard the bomb drop, that is when the danger was over.

Moreover, one direct hit on an inadequate shelter might have seriously increased the casualties.

3. The Defence has to ask: Is the advantage of saving a few hundred casualties sufficient to counterbalance the increased danger of panic from the sort of conditions described above by eyewitnesses? Is this not playing into the hands of the Attack by helping to create the conditions desired by the Attack?

To come to a reasonable decision as to whether a vast scheme of air-raid shelters would solve the needs of a city like London, we must remember first of all three general truths:

1. The object of the Attack is not to create casualties but to create panic. The Defence's primary duty, therefore, is to guard against

panic, and the reduction of casualties is a secondary consideration.

2. It is fallacious to imagine that air raids will be more or less predictable abnormalities. At the beginning of any war raids carried out according to the Technique of Silent Approach are likely to be the normal experience of London. Air-raid shelters will, therefore, be of little use unless people can stay in them for an unlimited number of hours, and even days.

3. Air-raid shelters must, therefore, be places in which people can work, and not simply become inactive. With these basic facts in our mind we see that the problem resolves itself into dividing up the population into those who can be helped by shelters and those who cannot, and as far as possible getting rid by evacuation of the latter.

The class-system of London during wartime will be very different from the normal. There will be three classes:

1. Those whose work is carried on in the open and whose work is essential to the continuance of civil and military life.

These include transport workers of all sorts, busmen, porters, delivery vanmen, milkmen, messenger-boys, dockers, policemen. They cannot be sent underground to wait for a few days or a week.

Consider the following note taken from an official of the Barcelona Junta de Defensa Pasiva:

"I am at the command of the Junta de Defensa Pasiva. We are always the first to arrive at places of disaster, and we need plenty of calm to resist the shock of the apocalyptic sights* we always see.

"We must advance firmly towards the mountain of ruins, without worrying about fresh falls of debris. Amid the clouds of dust and smoke we grope for the place whence the cries for help seem to come. We must locate the nearest as soon as possible and form chains of men to pass rapidly from hand to hand stones, pieces of mortar and

---

*In my notes I see that three people of very different stations all agree in describing their experiences as reminding them of the end of the world. Psychologists tell us that such fantasies are very often references to the beginnings of life rather than the end. It may be significant that conditions described in the form of birth fantasies lead on to panic.

metal until a space is opened to get at the victims.

"That's for victims in the top layers of the ruins. The most poignant drama comes next when we find living people below, who cannot be got out at once. Then our job lengthens into hours.

"One day, shortly after a raid, I went to help in the salvage of a children's school where nearly a hundred children were buried. We got out the living ones, and just as we were recovering some dead bodies another bomb fell near and the blood of the rescuers was mixed with the victims."

Nobody would suggest that people engaged on this work could be allowed to wait for hours in a bomb-proof shelter; but it must be remembered that the difference between their case and that of essential transport workers, policemen, busmen, and the rest is only a matter of degree.

What can be done for this class of the population? One thing only: their work must be reduced to the lowest essentials. All sorts of necessary movements, judged by peace standards, must be eliminated.

What will be needed is change in habits even more than structural precautions. Thus the diurnal migration of hundreds of thousands of office workers between work-place and suburbs will be unthinkable so long as the Technique of Silent Approach is a menace. It is not part of the essential minimum to which surface traffic must be limited.

2. The second class of the population will be those whose work is essential but capable of being carried on under cover.

Office workers, members of distributive trades, shop assistants, civil servants, so long as their work is necessary to war conditions, belong to this class. They can be provided with air-raid shelters, but it must be at the place where they work. They cannot be allowed to leave their work-places in order to burrow into the ground and become waiting, panic-breeding crowds. Every building capable of having its basement made into a bomb-proof dormitory must be commandeered for essential war services. Essential workers must sleep and eat where they work: they will be soldiers in the front-line trenches just as much in Kingsway or Lombard Street or Whitehall as anywhere else. When their turn for leave comes they will get out of London just as much as a soldier in Flanders got out of his trenches.

3. The third and largest class will be those whose work is inessential and whose presence plays into the hands of the Attack.

This includes the entire child population and a large proportion of the women. These cannot be put into shelters to wait hour after hour for the raids to be over. They must be evacuated at the very first moment. They are the target against which the Attack is aimed and their evacuation is the first step towards a successful reply to the Attack.

20

It would seem that whatever A.R.P. are contrived they must be such that they enable the community to keep moving and working. A hole in the ground is excellent if you are simply going to spend an odd half-hour in it. But let anyone who imagines this to be an adequate solution to the problem we have been set by the Attack remember that in Barcelona last March relays of half a dozen aeroplanes coming for about twenty-six minutes in all paralysed the life of a million and a half people for forty-odd hours. Such paralysis would be fatal even if sufficient excavations had been made to reduce the chances of sudden death to vanishing point. The community must move and work. There is another objection to the bomb-proof shelter. It costs an enormous sum to house the whole population in them and it is absolutely useless in time of peace. It should be obvious that the best way of spending money on A.R.P. would be in directions which would also give a dividend in peace-time.

Some money must be spent on projects with no peace-time use. There is the need for protective work on essential office buildings; zigzag trenches in all city parks and gardens may be necessary. But the major expense can fortunately be justified even if there is, after all, no war.

I suggest that the problems set by this new menace of Silent Approach can only be solved if large sums of money are spent on two precautions that have, very fortunately, a peace-time value.

Bearing in mind that the real problem is the forceful liquidating of peace-time social life and the immediate reconstruction of social life in a form capable of neutralizing the Attack, two chief measures are required:

(a) Evacuation. At present it is the habit of large classes of the population to migrate to the sea every year for a month. A.R.P. evacuation should be an extension of this. The immediate construction of summer camps complete with food dumps to which the entire child population of all big cities could be sent would give us preparedness for war, and would also do a great deal to make us less of a C_3 and more of an A nation.

If we are given a few more years, and if this summer school system is made to grow out of the existing functions of the Board of

I

Education, the war-time evacuation would lose much of its difficulty. It would not be subjecting a vast population to an abnormal strain, but rather to an extension of normal and pleasurable habit.

Naturally a government system of evacuation *en masse* could be supplemented by private enterprise, and many parents would prefer to arrange for their own evacuation. But a public system working through the schools must be the major objective, since time will be of the very essence of success.

(b) Once the non-essential population has been evacuated, the main object is to safeguard the movement of the city. Transport is the key industry before all others. Once more, since vast sums of money must be spent, it is fortunate that a peace-time need can be satisfied along with a war preparation.

All excavation must be, not in the service of passive waiting, but in the service of movement and work. A north-south and east-west subterranean highway linked to the underground railway system would be of enormous value to London's peace-time traffic problem, and in war would maintain the life of the city more effectively than the largest imaginable system of bomb-proof shelters.

In the first place, subterranean highways would circumvent the very serious problem of surface transport obstruction. London will be in a far worse position than Barcelona in this respect, and every effort must be made to leave the streets free for essentials, such as fire-fighting services.*

In the second place, safe storage and shelter can grow out of a system of subterranean communications without the psychological and physical disadvantages to which we have referred.

In the third place, the construction of these toll roads, as they would be in peace-time, would not be mere wasting of money on the necessary folly of war. In a few weeks it is probable that attrition or the discovery of efficient counter-measures by the Active

---

*I am told on excellent authority that the fire risk in London is greater than in any other European capital owing to the crowding in some areas of highly inflammable buildings in narrow streets.

Defence would make the Technique of Silent Approach obsolete. We would still have our summer camps and our vastly improved transport system instead of a large number of holes in the ground with no peace-time meaning whatever.

Moreover, we should have solved the problem set by the Attack, whereas the bomb-proof shelter in itself does not solve it. We should have maintained activity and movement against all attempts to paralyse them.

21

This has been a technical study of the A.R.P. lessons we should learn from the Italo-German manœuvres over Barcelona last March. Political considerations have not entered into it.

It is certainly no part of the author's task to discover whether the present Government is to blame for inadequate A.R.P. That A.R.P. are not as yet adequate is as plain to the Government authorities as it can be to anyone else. Nor can he discuss the question whether or no any Government should be supported or hindered in its efforts to make the community A.R.P. conscious. There is a political school of thought which dismisses the whole thing as an attempt on the Government's part to 'militarize the minds of the people.' These will no doubt oppose the idea of summer camps on the ground that they may be used to turn children into soldiers.

Nearly all this, but not quite all, is outside the scope of this book; though it is only fair to say that anyone who has seen actualities in Barcelona is likely to be impatient with those who believe that democracies should allow themselves to be bombed into panic without trying to save themselves.

There is, however, one political idea which is also a technical one, and which therefore is relevant to a technical study. There are some people optimistic or pessimistic enough —according to the reader's political colour-ing—to believe that the psychological effect of an air raid is likely to be a movement of intelligent protest against a Government so incapable of governing as to be powerless to prevent such a calamity.

It is often suggested by those who hold this belief that the sole interest of the present Government is to avoid such indignation and that they are sacrificing all other considerations to this.

It may be said at once that if our A.R.P. policy is designed solely to avoid the Government falling into disfavour, it is conceived in a highly incompetent manner. Indeed, the main criticism that one is likely to make of the official policy, especially after studying actualities in Spain, is that it is fraught with danger to public order. It is giving the public a quite incorrect picture of the reality, and nothing is likely to be more dangerous to a Government in the long run than the discovery that it has not prepared for the reality when it comes.

It seems more likely that the Government is ignorant rather than Machiavellian. The only real lesson the world has yet had of a European city being bombed under conditions relevant to London was the Barcelona manœuvres of last March. There has scarcely been time yet for that lesson to percolate through official machinery.

Now, is there any evidence that anti-Government feeling will be set up by an air raid? Naturally, this depends on the Government and its relationship to the community as a whole.

In Spain there has been a progression of feeling of some interest. When, early in the war, warships of unknown nationality bombarded the small fishing village of Rosas, north of Barcelona, the uncontrolled extremists, who had a great deal of power in those days, reacted by immediately shooting a large number of Fascist prisoners. If Barcelona had been raided then, the few thousand Fascists and suspected Fascists in the city would have been shot out of hand. Now that discipline has been firmly re-established by the Spanish Government, no such reprisals are possible.

On the other hand, the immediate effect on the few Fascist sympathizers in Barcelona that I was able to sound out was to weaken their sympathies. "My philo-Fascist friends," someone said, "always try to find a 'military objective' near any bomb that falls, but when the bomb falls near them they say, 'I know there's a railway line here, but why can't the *hijos de putas* bomb the line farther up?'" The knowledge that it is foreigners who are bombing Spain has a particularly violent effect on the Spanish reaction to air-raids, but always the natural reaction of anyone to a raid is hatred against the pilots as men, whatever their side may be. As the British Conservative M.P. said during a Madrid raid when some Soviet pursuit planes flew over his head: "Thank God they are *ours*."

It is true that if we find ourselves being bombed from the air, Sir Oswald Mosley and his followers will probably have to be given police protection; but this first stage where the reaction is perfectly reasonable anger rapidly passes into another stage. It seems that Silent Approach does not make people angry: it disintegrates them down to a far lower level of incoherence.

This is not the place to attempt a technical

definition of panic. The reader may be referred to Dr. Rickman's article for this. I shall content myself with piecing together evidence gathered from Barcelona into a layman's picture of psychological actualities.

In normal life a butterfly satisfies its categorical need to reproduce itself according to an elaborate plan; the eggs are laid when fertile, at the right time, on the right part of the right food plant.

Put that same butterfly into a cyanide bottle. In its death agony the categorical need does not disappear although none of the necessary conditions are present, and although the eggs may not have been fertilized, although no plant is there, the dying butterfly uselessly lays its eggs.

This is a simple analogy of what happens to a man subjected to the Technique of Silent Approach with High Explosive. There are certain basic actions, some with a biological meaning, others due to the complication that man is a social animal invisibly tied to his fellows; these only have a meaning when the conditions are right, and man uses his power of conscious thought to limit his bodily reactions to occasions when conditions give those reactions a real meaning.

The air raid stuns the man's power of conscious thought, but not his body's power of action, nor his unconscious needs tying him to his fellows. These continue, but now they are unguided; his body wastes its energy on futilities, he is sick, he runs about, he stops still, but whatever it may be that his body does, it is useless as a means of coping with the dangerous situation. Here is an eyewitness account of this:

"Suddenly we heard explosions and at once the anti-aircraft guns opened up. At the same moment panic broke loose as the people scattered crazily in all directions, plunging into doorways, falling over and over.

"Four or five thousand metres high appeared three or four aluminium-coloured planes. They seemed to be directly overhead. I saw a group of people who had run up a small alleyway bordered by two high walls. They pressed themselves against these walls. They sprang from one side to the other in the crazy belief that the wall opposite would give more protection than the one they had left.

"Meanwhile they looked up at the planes and, according to the impression they got of the position of the planes in the sky, they moved from one side to the other of the alleyway. Some continued running down the alley. They were running away from bombers who were speeding along at three hundred miles an hour. Two minutes later the bombers were out of sight and the people calm again."

So much for the panic effects on bodily action. What of the psychological effects? What happens to the social needs suddenly left unsatisfied? I regret that as I have to confine myself to observed facts, I can only suggest the negative observation that whatever new ties may be formed between one person and another to take the place of those so roughly broken, they do not get the chance of functioning on an intellectual plane.

Panic does not help people to band

together to carry out an intelligent construc-
tive revolution; it leaves them bewildered,
and content to carry out the mechanical
duties of facing scarcity and the miseries of
war. In such circumstances any Government, however vile, has little to fear from
the anger of its people, but any Government,
however good, has everything to fear from
their being stunned into inaction or futile
unco-ordinated action.

What happens later is another matter, and
we cannot go into it here. But it is worth
repeating that nobody has anything to gain
from inefficient A.R.P., and that a democracy
can only save itself by assisting its Government to make them efficient at whatever
cost. Whether or no, once the Attack has
been defeated, the democracy will have to
save itself from its own Government is
quite another matter. For the moment the
important point for all to realize is that it
is Fascists who bomb civilian populations
from the air and that they must be stopped.

And the time for action is now. Unfortu-
nately, there is a dangerous attitude towards

A.R.P. to be observed on all sides. People seem to have persuaded themselves that 'nothing is any good anyhow' and that they will therefore do nothing. It must be confessed that the very low level of intelligence shown by many lecturers on A.R.P., and a partially justifiable feeling that there has been too much talk about useless measures of protection, is responsible for this.

Such scepticism is fatal. We must act, and act now, if democratic defence is to put up a show against totalitarian attack. Fortunately, as I have tried to show, our action can combine the amelioration of peace-time living with preparation for war defence. When public opinion is alive to the possibilities of a real A.R.P. programme it will demand a lead from the Government that shall be more inspiring than anything that we have yet been given.

A programme of summer camps that can later be used if necessary for evacuation and of traffic improvements which will be a blessing in peace, as well as a safeguard in war—this would inspire more enthusiasm

PLATE I

PLATE II

PLATE III

PLATE IV

PLATE V

PLATE VI

PLATE VII

PLATE VIII

PLATE IX

PLATE X

PLATE XI

PLATE XII

PLATE XIII

PLATE XIV

PLATE XV

PLATE XVI

PLATE XVII

PLATE XVIII

PLATE XIX

PLATE XX

PLATE XXI

PLATE XXII

PLATE XXIII

PLATE XXIV

PLATE XXV

PLATE XXVI

PLATE XXVII

PLATE XXVIII

PLATE XXIX

PLATE XXX

PLATE XXXI

PLATE XXXII